31 Steps to Show Your Love

Philip Vang

Copyright 2014 - Philip Vang

Contents

Contents

1 Introduction

I want to thank you and congratulate you for getting the book, "31 Steps to Show Your Love: This Ultimate Guide Will Show You Creative Ideas. This Will Improve Your Relationship With Your Partner, Spouse, Wife or Husband and Pave the Way to a Stronger Future Together".

Are you in a relationship where you noticed you two are drifting apart? Have a difficult time? Or just want to improve what you have? I noticed that showing your love to your partner without expecting a response right away will greatly improve the relationship and your partner will surly notice the gestures sooner rather than later. Thus building a much more powerful relationship.

Thanks again for getting this book, I hope you enjoy it!

Sincerely,

Philip Vang

Author of 31 Steps to Show Your Love

2 Publisher's Note

Care has been taken to confirm the accuracy of the information presented and to describe generally accepted practices. However, the authors, editors, and publisher are not responsible for errors or omissions or for any consequences from application of the information in this book and make no warranty, express or implied, with respect to the contents of the publication.

The authors, editors, and publisher have exerted every effort to ensure that any drug selection and dosage set forth in this text are in accordance with current recommendations and practice at the time of publication. However, in view of ongoing research, changes in government regulations, and the constant flow of information relating to drug therapy and drug reactions, the reader is urged to check the package insert for each drug for any change in indications and dosage and for added warnings and precautions. This is particularly important when the recommended agent is a new or infrequently employed drug.

Some drugs and medical devices presented in this publication may have Food and Drug Administration (FDA) clearance for limited use in restricted research settings. It is the responsibility of the health care provider to ascertain the FDA status of each drug or device planned for use in their clinical practice.

3 Step 1: Give Your Partner a Few Compliments

Giving your special someone sincere compliments shows that you notice their efforts and strengths. They may have gone through the entire day or week without being complimented so it is important to show them that they still impress you. Your romantic partner wants to impress you when they have the chance to do so. As a good wife or girlfriend, you have to appreciate their efforts. However, be careful in choosing your words. You may mean no harm, but they may interpret it the other way around and be insulted instead. Men are more sensitive to words that will hurt their male ego. Here are a few lines to avoid.

- "That's sweet, but it's OK. I can do it faster." Do you mean he's slow at it?
- "I'm so shocked that you were able to fix it." So you think he can't?
- "Thanks for trying." "Trying" means he did a bad job.

4 Step 2: Try New Things Together

Emotional bond between two people, regardless of gender, occurs through shared experiences that involve intense, positive emotions. That is how people make good friendships. In your relationship, you can show your love by trying new things together. This does not just mean eating in an exciting new restaurant, although it counts as one. You need to show that you're not willing to get stuck in a boring, monotonous routine. Doing something adventurous with your romantic partner displays that you consider them as your first choice if you want to have fun. If you two are busy professionals, you can always find time in a week to do something adventurous together. It can be as simple as checking out a museum of weird things, hiking or cycling. Do you like to do something adventurous with someone you're emotionally distant? Trying something new with your partner shows that you're not emotionally distant from them.

5 Step 3: Be Romantic

Being romantic seems like an obvious part of a relationship, but believe it or not most couples fail to be romantic once they are a few months deep into their relationship. It is a sad fact that drives "committed" men and women to cheat in order to feel appreciated or loved again. Many couples are also busy with their careers so it can be hard to squeeze a romantic time into their schedules. But is your busy schedule really worth losing your partner to other people who are starting to appreciate your partner more than you do? If not, do a few romantic gestures. How did you feel when you and your romantic partner first started dating? Recall the feeling of infatuation and imagine how you always tried to look your best. Have a candle light dinner as a surprise. If your partner loves you, they will appreciate it.

6 Step 4: Give Them Gifts

The basic gist of showing your love to your romantic partner depends on how you appreciate them no matter how long you have been together. In your first few dates together, you were fond of giving each other gifts. Now, you may find yourselves ignorant to gift giving unless it is your "monthsary", anniversary and birthday. Rekindle the youthful feeling of infatuation by giving each other sincere gifts. Giving gifts is also symbolic; it shows that the recipient is special. Most people don't have the energy to spend time and money on someone who does not matter. Show that your romantic partner is worth your time, effort and money by surprising them with gifts from time to time. It doesn't have to be an expensive watch or jewelry. It could be a simple casing for their gadgets or a few tools and accessories for their car.

7 Step 5: Spice Up Your Sex Life

Sex is an essential part of every romantic relationship. However, some couples choose to abstain from sex before they are married. If you're not one of these couples, you have to keep your sex life as interesting as possible. Boring and meaningless sex is one of the many factors why men and women in a relationship cheat. The desire for sex is one of the base human needs, just like hunger. It is also normal for two people to have a bland sex life once they have been together for several months or years. Either of you may find one another not as attractive as before. As a woman, perhaps you may have started to think of sex as a routine. Introduce something new to the bedroom such as sex toys, fuzzy handcuffs, flavored lubricants and vibrating cock rings.

You might also be interested in another great book we have published called "31 Steps to Better Sex". You can download it over at amazon with this link: http://bit.ly/31bettersex

8 Step 6: Basic Hugs and Kisses

Hugs and kisses are the best way to show your love to your romantic partner every day. You're free to kiss and hug them whenever they're around. Kiss and hug your partner before they go to bed and before they leave for work. Greet them good morning and good night everyday and seal your greetings with a kiss and a hug. Unlike compliments, hugs and kisses can never be misinterpreted because they are universal expressions of affection. Whether you're at home or on the streets, you can always sneak a kiss for your special someone. If you romantic partner is not comfortable with public display of affection, you can simply hold hands. You can also wrap your hands across their waist to show affection even more. When you're at home, never fail to hug and kiss them.

9 Step 7: Surprise, Surprise!

Earlier, it was mentioned that giving your romantic partner surprise presents from time to time is a healthy way to show your love. Showing your romantic partner random surprise should not end in random presents. You can make a surprise breakfast in bed for them with their favorite breakfast. You could also trail Post It's with short notes leading to a final surprise. This could lead to a sultry bath with candle lights and champagne or a romantic candle light dinner with music. It would only be a pleasant surprise if you know what they want. Of the many months you've been together, remembering what they want shows that you pay attention to them. Maybe you've noticed them stopping by at the grocery to pick up their comfort food (ice cream, chocolate bar, etc). Whatever your surprise is, it should be something you know they'd like.

10 Step 8: Make Their Life a Bit Easier

Nobody wants to see their loved one having a hard time. Likewise, you don't want to see your romantic partner going through his day with a lot of difficulty, especially if they are the breadwinner. Show your love to them by offering your help. You don't have to volunteer about something you're not really knowledgeable about, like for example, offering to fix their car or do some serious work-related help. But you can help them by offering what you're good at, but this does not mean doing everything for them. It can be simple things like laying out their clothes for work tomorrow or sorting the mail. If both of you have your own busy careers, then it's just fair that he or she would also do something to make your life a little bit easier. Your partner can offer a help in the kitchen, wash the dishes, do the laundry so you can relax a little bit.

11 Step 9: Learn to Cook for Them

There is probably no person in the planet who does not love a good meal cooked by his wife or girlfriend. The saying goes that a way to a man's heart is through his stomach; this won't be a saying for no reason. Most people cook something special only on certain occasions such as Thanksgiving, Christmas and New Year. Why not cook something special for your romantic partner even if there is no occasion? You can either cook them a special breakfast or dinner. They will love coming home to you after a very stressful day knowing that something special is prepared on the table. To make it even more special, prepare desserts. If you don't have time to prepare a sumptuous dinner, you can opt to bake a cake instead or make some cookies.

12 Step 10: Show Your Support

Most adults are under a lot of pressure to prove that they are worthy and successful. Moreover, they don't like appearing like a failure to you and of course, their parents. Plus there could be a silent competition among your partner's siblings. If they're the eldest, they could even be in a lot deeper pressure to be successful. If you're more successful than them in your respective field or if you earn more than they do, their ego can be hurt a bit, especially if you're with a man. Show your love for your partner by supporting them in their endeavors and dreams. Someone who loves you will talk about their dreams with you because they are not afraid to open up. Don't betray their trust in you by belittling his dreams and goals.

13 Step 11: They Hate It? Don't Force Them

It is OK for your partner to help you with something (chores, work load, etc.). But to be honest, they like doing none of these things. They only do them for you. It's also totally fine for you to help them even if you don't really like doing those things. However, if your romantic partner hates doing something, don't force them to do it. Don't even think about blackmailing them to do it as a proof that he loves you. If they volunteer to do the a few tasks, why not? But don't shun of their efforts by saying "I can do it better." Guide them through it and they will slowly learn, although not as perfect as you do. Teaching them how to do something can also serve as a bonding time for the two of you. Remember to thank them for making an effort and kiss them afterwards.

14 Step 12: Try to Learn What They Love

You will be with your romantic partner for quite a long time, provided that both of you genuinely love each other. With that said, it is impossible for the two of you not to be involved with each other's hobbies and activities. When you love someone, you will become curious about what they do. In this case, it will be natural and even automatic for you to become curious about what your romantic partner loves. A person who loves you truly would be flattered by your gesture of taking interest with what they love to do. If your romantic partner is into sports, try to learn about their favorite team. Ask them questions (just not during the game) such as what made him prefer that team. If they're into arts and crafts, schedule a craft session together.

15 Step 13: Be Crazy Together

Doing crazy things together brings back your youthful days. Subconsciously, both you and your romantic partner have a silent but deep longing to be young again. When men and women feel bored in their relationships, no matter how committed they appear to be, they will seek ways in order to feel refreshed and revived. Cheating on a younger woman, for example, is part of a person's way to find their youthful self back. Once in a while, do something fun but harmless such as dedicating songs to each other on the radio, hide a love note in their luggage when they're leaving for a business trip, have a t-shirt or pillow customized with your personalized message for them, go have a footspa, manicure and pedicure together, etc. There are countless of new and crazy things to do for couples online so make sure to search for them.

16 Step 14: Communicate Well

You have probably already learned that they are not great when decoding women's verbal signals. Women, on the other hand, tend to exaggerate something when it's unclear to them. A good communication is one of the building blocks of a good relationship. Without this, you cannot reach into each other. Show your love to your romantic partner by honing good communication skills. Sure, this step may not be so romantic, but it will help clear your relationship of any hidden resentment or problems. This may be difficult but as much as possible, avoid the silent treatment. If you don't feel like talking to your partner, tell them you need a while to clear your thoughts and let your anger dissipate. Talk about how their actions make you feel, not about what they should do.

17 Step 15: Be Honest

There are good lies and bad lies. In a romantic relationship, it's important to keep everything true because sooner or later, the other party will uncover the lies, even if you reason that it's for their own good. Being honest may cause temporary pains and problems, but it will save you from feeling guilty. As we all know, guilt becomes obvious through body language. Another benefit of being honest to your romantic partner is that you would never have to memorize any lies therefore allowing you to be consistent with what you say to them. If you dislike something they did, tell them honestly but thoughtfully. In the end, suggest an alternative but leave the options open so they won't feel being dictated.

18 Step 16: Compromise Once in a While

You and your romantic partner are not carbon copies of each other; therefore there would be differences in your preferences, abilities and attitudes. Show your love to your romantic partner by learning how to compromise once in a while. However, your partner should pick up on your efforts and should also compromise for you, too, when you need it. Compromising shows that you factor your romantic partner in your decisions. When you're deciding about something that doesn't quite fit both of you, sit and discuss matters with them. List all the pros and cons of your options. If you have children, factor them in your decision making as well. Both of you should compromise to show respect for one another.

19 Step 17: Don't Roast Them Over Past Relationships

It is completely normal that you may not be your partner's first romantic encounter. As a result, they will inevitably talk about their ex lovers in the future. As long as they have healed from his past relationships, there is no reason to be jealous. Don't accuse them of cheating just because they are kind their exes. Show your love to your romantic partner by being confident about his trust and love for you. Don't panic that they might fall back in love with their ex just because he ran into them. Don't go crazy if you see them talking together. Just make sure that they are not talking intimately with each other. If they have plans to meet up, your partner should tell you about it.

20 Step 18: Don't Be Overly Jealous

There are almost 7 billion people all over the world. Your romantic partner will encounter a few hundred men and women in a lifetime, some of which will become their friends. If you're with a man, some of their female friends may even be gorgeous enough to make you wonder why he chose you and not one of them. Show your love to your romantic partner by having faith in your relationship. If you're overly jealous, your partner would get annoyed and may even avoid you because you're beginning to get too toxic for them. Don't go crazy if you see them talking casually to another. Respect their female friends no matter how insecure they may make you feel.

21 Step 19: Don't Judge Their Friends

Your romantic partner chose their friends. Judging them would hurt your partner's feelings because in a way, they care for them, too. They have a silent but deep bond with among their close peers. If you judge one of them, your partner may not only feel hurt but also dislike you gradually. Don't prohibit them to hang out with their friends. This will create an impression that you're a suffocating, possessive girlfriend that won't let him have any fun outside of your relationship. Your time together is important. Likewise, their time with their friends is important, too. Their friends are a source of companionship and network. Don't blatantly say anything negative about them. Friendships that last for years are rare so let your partner have it.

22 Step 20: Be Positive

There is something very attractive with positive people. It's as if they have a radiant, glowing aura around them. Positive people make other people feel hopeful about the future. Simply put, positive people are not toxic to be with. In a serious relationship, it is often inevitable to encounter serious problems especially if you're married. Avoid whining and nagging. If your partner constantly hears you nagging and whining, they would assume that they are doing terrible in everything. The two of you should be a team. Team members have a common goal and they don't let each other down. Smile as much as possible. Show off your sense of humor (only when appropriate) to keep things light. Be a shoulder to lean on when your partner is feeling emotionally down.

23 Step 21: Give Them Some Private Time

The quality of time spend together contributes to your bond as a couple. The more time you have known each other before you started dating, the higher the chances your relationship is going to last. However, your romantic partner will need some time for themselves occasionally. They love you, but it does not mean that you have to be there every second of their lives. They would love to go home to you, but you don't have to check on their whereabouts. Give your partner some time for himself. Let them play his favorite video games, watch his favorite movies and spend a night out with their friends. When they truly love you, cheating would meet their mind with disgust so don't be alarmed. Just have them inform you what time he'd be home for their own safety.

24 Step 22: Be Considerate

There will be times in your relationship with your romantic partner that he would fail to please you. There will also be times where they don't feel like getting intimate and may want to be alone for a while. This usually happens when they are facing problems at work. Don't press them to talk if they're not yet ready. Just be there and prepare yourself emotionally. In today's unstable and almost unpredictable economy, it's hard to say that one would be financially secured through employment. Be considerate with your romantic partner if they're having difficulties at work. If they have health problems, help them to find a cure instead of blaming them. They look at you as someone they can trust so show your love to them by being considerate.

25 Step 23: Write a Short Letter

Almost everything today is done digitally; it is more convenient and it takes less space. However, there are aspects of your relationship that are better expressed through meaningful objects. Writing a letter to your romantic partner is one of them. You can express how thankful you're that you have met them and how significantly enjoyable they made your existence to be. Whatever you decide to write, write it sincerely. You can also print out a couple of pictures of you together and caption them. You can also draw and doodle if you want to. Write legibly using a pen instead of printing a letter to make it appear more personal. Express your simple yet fun and artistic side. If you want, you can dab your perfume on the letter so the scent would remind them of you.

26 Step 24: Speak With Your Eyes

Words may convey meaning, but eyes express what your words might have missed. Couples who have been together for several months have the habit of communicating to each other without looking into each other's eyes. They are so used to each other's presence that they are starting to take it for granted. When you first started dating, you may recall that you can't stop looking at each other and your attention is always directed to him when they're speaking and vice versa. Show your love to your romantic partner by rekindling this kind of attention. When you're happy to see them, show your joy through your eyes and look at their eyes and smile. When you're feeling sensual, give a seductive look with your eyes. When they're telling how their day went, look them in the eye and show your interest.

27 Step 25: Pay Attention to Your Body Language

Your body language may be the hardest thing to control because it comes naturally. You will unconsciously tilt your torso away from someone you dislike and cross your arms in disagreement. When you're interested with someone, you will let your hips and pelvis turn towards them. In addition, you may also imitate their body language. Also, you will notice yourself leaning forward a bit and raising both of your eyebrows as you speak with a smile. All of this happens automatically. If you're always turning your back to your romantic partner, even in bed, they may think that you're losing interest. Look up for a list of body language cues that show interest and you'll find a lot which you can use to show your love and interest to your romantic partner.

28 Step 26: Touch Them Sincerely

Nothing indicates that you're intimate more than physical touches. Unlike kind words and compliments, touching them elicits their attention automatically because instinctively, people are conscious about their personal space for their protection. The normal spacing between two casual people when talking to each other is usually 1.5 to 2 feet. Break this casual status by touching your partner. According to David Givens, the director of the Center for Nonverbal Studies in Spokane, Washington, "If seeing is believing, touching is knowing." The brain processes touching faster than words and as a result, your partner feels more comforted with light caresses than kind words. Adults are considered as "touch deprived." They would feel comforted when special loved one touches them, whether it is in the form of hugs and pats. To show your love better, add physical touches.

29 Step 27: Pamper Each Other

Adults nowadays are busier than ever. Technology has also contributed with the decline of personal communication. At the end of the day, this keeps most people feeling exhausted and even unloved. Show your love to your romantic partner by pampering him. To make the experience better and more meaningful, let him pamper you, too. People are drawn to something (or someone) that makes them feel comfortable and happy. If you make your partner feel happy, you'd be irresistible. Here is a short list to give you an idea:

- When they come home from work, invite them for a massage. Neatly set up a clean towel over the bed (to protect the bed sheet from massage oils), diffuse some fragrance oils and light a few candles.
- Prepare a sumptuous dinner.
- Invite them for a couples' massage.
- Have a warm and relaxing bath together.

30 Step 28: Treasure Your Memories Together

As sad as it sounds, nobody is promised tomorrow. Yet, people go on with their lives as if they're super sure that they'll live for another year. It may sound inappropriate but one day, you and your romantic partner will have to rest. Show your love to your partner by treasuring the moments you had together. Take lots of pictures (don't post everything online), print them and craft them into scrap books or cards. You can even make a collage and frame a few of your favorite pictures. Write the date at the back or in the corner. Record family occasions on video. Make personalized mementos (keychains, bracelets, pendants, etc) and keep it inside a special "memories box". Write down special dates (your first attempts together, etc). On your anniversary or on Valentine's, open this box and see how far you've come in your relationship.

31 Step 29: Thank Them

People often forget to thank others when they become accustomed to them. It is as if they are ought to do favors without being recognized. As your partner's special someone, you must show them appreciation more than anybody else. Make it a habit in your romantic relationship to always thank each other. If your romantic partner brought home dinner, thank them with a smile and a kiss. Show that you really appreciate it. If you two have children, set an example of being grateful. Before going to sleep, write the things that you're grateful for that day. This will help you feel more satisfied and fulfilled in your relationship. If you want to get creative, you can make or buy a card and list the things you want to thank them for.

32 Step 30: Keep Your Fights Private

There are some things which you must only discuss between yourselves. This is a way of showing respect to your relationship. Don't argue rashly in public that involves shouting and pushing each other. Respect each other as much as you respect your relationship. Petty fights and arguments belong to a healthy relationship. With the advent of social media, it is tempting to vent online but as much as possible, avoid it. What you post online stays in the internet even if you delete it. Your friends and parents don't have to know everything that goes on in your relationship. Don't involve them in your quarrels as a couple. When you fight, aim to resolve the problem. Argue your side and let them defend their, but make sure to direct your argument to a middle ground where you can agree with each other. If you're wrong, learn to apologize.

33 Step 31: Say "I Love You"

Say "I love you" rather than "love ya." There is a big difference between the two. Omitting the personal pronoun "I" makes it sound insincere. These three words should be special, so avoid saying them when you don't really mean it. If you have been together for several months or years now, you may find it unnecessary to tell your romantic partner that you love them. Why should you when your efforts already "speak" that you love them? Ask yourself, are you really doing those out of love or routine? They may not immediately interpret your efforts as love so it's still important to tell them how much you love them. Look into their eyes as you do so and then touch and kiss them. He should feel a deep connection to you as you do this.

34 Closing Thoughts

I hope you enjoyed the read and found what you were looking for. If so, I'd like to ask you for a favor: Please, take a moment to **review my book on Amazon!** Thanks.

Thank you for getting "31 Steps to Show Your Love" and I wish you an amazing relationship. Have fun together and build on strong basis.

If you would like to get updates about special offers and new books from me or see my other books, please visit my author profile at our publisher website:

publishedok.com/pv

Philip Vang

Author

35 Preview of "31 Steps to a Better YouTube Channel"

Preview chapter of "31 Steps to a Better YouTube Channel: Optimize Your Channel, Make More Money, Gain Subscribers, Audience and Views. This Ultimate Guide Will Help You To Make A Living of YouTube":

When recording your video, make sure that you are doing the right thing. Here are some tips that you can take into consideration when filming:

- Do not use digital zoom because the camera uses the highest optical zoom available and then crops the image to a smaller portion of the scene. Therefore, the camcorder is redrawing pixels.

- Make sure that the subject of your videos (i.e. yourself) is properly exposed. You may opt to set the exposure manually, most especially if the subject is backlight.
- Never, ever pan too fast or too slow. If you pan the video too quickly, the details will not be seen. On the other hand, if you pan it too slowly, the video will appear boring.
- Keep your camera steady. Nobody wants to watch a shaky video (unless there is an earthquake in the scene). Therefore, it is important to keep your camera steady to avoid shaking. The most common option that you have is to use a tripod. However, if you do not have a tripod, you can just place your camera on a steady surface like a table.
- ...

Preview of the Table of Contents of "31 Steps to a Better YouTube Channel":

- Write a Description About Your Channel
- Leave Comments on Other YouTuber's Videos
- Send Messages to Other People on YouTube
- Choose the Right Camera
- Get the Right Equipment
- Come Up With Ideas
- Record Your Video

To check out the rest of "31 Steps to a Better YouTube Channel: Optimize Your Channel, Make More Money, Gain Subscribers, Audience and Views. This Ultimate Guide Will Help You To Make A Living of YouTube" please visit the following link:

bit.ly/31youtube

36 Preview of "31 Steps to Become a Vegan"

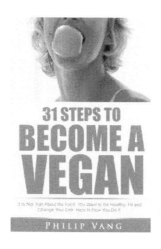

Preview chapter of "31 Steps to Become a Vegan: It Is Not Just About the Food. You Want to Be Healthy, Fit and Change Your Diet. Here Is How You Do It.":

A great way to start off your vegan plan of action is to ease into it. This will make the choice much easier, if the adjustment is made not abruptly, but gradually. The transition of your body will also be easy. Any sudden, drastic change in your diet will affect your body tremendously, especially changes in being an omnivore to becoming a full-pledged vegan.

One thing to remember is to listen to what your body is telling you and avoid forcing yourself to change everything completely without proper guidance and information. You may start by removing cheese, then eggs, then milk and dairy products, then meat. It is also advisable to remove one type of animal from your diet at a time. One can also start with being vegetarian, then removing eggs and dairy eventually. The most important thing is to go at your own pace. You may also begin with one thing that you consume the most, and then start substituting with the vegan version.

For instance, if you drink milk every day, you may begin substituting it with almond milk. One great way of doing it is taking into account all the junk food in your home, such as anything with refined flour, sugar and processed food. One may target one type of junk food and start with a healthier vegan option. If you have potato chips and cheese dip, why not have some nacho cheese and salsa. If you like candy, why not eat apples and bananas?

It takes months, even years to build a habit, so a gradual approach is always the better choice. Going cold turkey is like setting yourself up for failure.

Preview of the Table of Contents of "31 Steps to Become a Vegan":

- Research and Plan Your Vegan Journey
- Start It Right
- Know What Vegans Eat
- Eating and Cooking Vegan Good
- Living Vegan
- Sustaining the Vegan Lifestyle

To check out the rest of "31 Steps to Become a Vegan: It Is Not Just About the Food. You Want to Be Healthy, Fit and Change Your Diet. Here Is How You Do It." please visit the following link:

bit.ly/31vegan

37 Preview of "31 Steps to Start a Business"

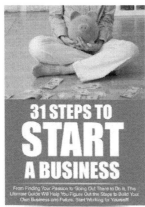

PHILIP VANG

Preview chapter of "31 Steps to Start a Business: From Finding Your Passion to Going Out There to Do It, This Ultimate Guide Will Help You Figure Out the Steps to Build Your Own Business and Future. Start Working for Yourself!":

In managing a business, there lies a huge difference between "you have to" and "you want to". The first one dictates that you are obliged to accomplish something even if you see no reason of doing it. You are forced to complete a task that in return, produces poor outcomes. Mediocre outputs may mean downfall to the business since the customers always want the best products and services.

In order to generate better results, doing what you want helps you achieve this goal. Recognizing your passions can definitely help you attain success in your endeavor. Additionally, identifying the purpose of your business can aid you in continuing what you have established. Reminding of yourself why you started in the first place may inspire you to carry on with your venture. In the long run, you will realize that managing a business is easier when you are motivated.

Preview of the Table of Contents of "31 Steps to Start a Business":

- Evaluating Yourself
- Identifying Your Passion
- Establishing Your Goal
- Devising Your Business Plan
- Choosing Your Business Structure
- Recognizing Your Target Market
- Calculating the Costs
- Fixing Your Budget
- Gathering Your Resources
- Obtaining a Place of Work

To check out the rest of "31 Steps to Start a Business: From Finding Your Passion to Going Out There to Do It, This Ultimate Guide Will Help You Figure Out the Steps to Build Your Own Business and Future. Start Working for Yourself!" please visit the following link:

bit.ly/31business

Made in the USA
San Bernardino, CA
09 January 2017